CRICKET—HOW TO PLAY

PLAY THE GAME SERIES

CRICKET– HOW TO PLAY

Published for the
N C A

E.P. PUBLISHING LTD.
Bradford Road, East Ardsley,
Wakefield, Yorkshire, WF3 2JN, England.

First Edition 1955
Reprinted 1955
Second Edition 1957
Reprinted 1958
Third Edition 1961
Reprinted 1965
Revised 1969
Published by
E.P. PUBLISHING LTD.
Bradford Road,
East Ardsley, Wakefield,
Yorkshire, WF3 2JN,
England.

7158 0151 1

© E.P. Publishing Ltd., 1969.
World Copyright Reserved

Printed in Great Britain by
DIXON & STELL LTD., CROSS HILLS, Nr. KEIGHLEY.

FOREWORD

Every young cricketer who wants to improve his game must be prepared to think about it and work at it. There is no easy road to success. Cricket is a hard task-master: it demands common-sense, imagination, concentration and character.

There will, and always should, be variety and individuality in the way cricketers bat, bowl and field, but there must also be certain basic principles in each sphere of the game which the young player must try to understand, to practise and to master if he is to make the best of his natural gifts.

The first aim of this book is to analyse and illustrate these. But it is also concerned with what is equally important, the mental approach to the game: for unless that is right, no natural gifts, no technical skill, will command lasting success.

No real cricketer should ever stop learning: the more he learns and the harder he works at it, the better he will play the game and the more he will enjoy it.

CONTENTS

	Page
Foreword	5
The Approach to the Game	8
Equipment	9
The Meaning of Length	10

BATTING

The Grip	15
The Stance	18
The Back Lift	20
Forward Strokes	22
The Drives	26
The Back Stroke in Defence	36
The Attacking Back Stroke	38
Horizontal Back Strokes	40
The Leg Glances	50
Running Between the Wickets	52
Playing an Innings	53
Net Practice	54

BOWLING

The Basic Action	57
Spin Bowling	64
Swerve	67
Bowling Tactics	69
The Fast Bowler	70
The Medium Pace Bowler	71
The Spin Bowler	72

FIELDING

Stopping the Ball	74
Attacking Fielding	75
The Throw	78
The Close-In Fielders	80
Catching	80

WICKET KEEPING

Equipment	83
Position	83
Stance	84
Taking the Ball	85
Stumping	87
Taking Returns from the Field	87
Practice	87

CAPTAINCY

Off the Field	88
Out in the Field	89
From the Pavilion	90

UMPIRING

The L.B.W. Law	93

THE APPROACH TO THE GAME

Cricket has been played in England for at least 400 years and probably, in a primitive form, for very much longer. In the last century it has, like Puck in *The Midsummer's Night Dream*, fetched a girdle round the earth, so that today it can be truly said that the sun never sets upon the game.

Every boy therefore, who plays it today is the heir to a great English tradition and can help to hand on and even to enrich this part of the English way of life.

He will obviously want to play as well as he can, and this book has been written in the hope that it may help him to do so.

But there is something that matters even more than making runs or taking wickets or being a good fielder.

A cricketer should never forget that he is playing with, as well as against the other team and that he is either their host or their guest.

He should strive for all that he is worth to win or, if he cannot win, to avert defeat; but there is a price beyond which victory or the avoidance of defeat should never be bought.

For in cricket, however hard it is played—and if it is worth playing at all, it is worth playing hard—the struggle and its result should never obscure the true ends for which it is played, recreation, good fellowship, the training of character, and above all the conviction which the game can bring that, through it and what it gives, life is indeed the more worth living.

EQUIPMENT

Every cricketer should take pride in turning out as smart and tidy as he can and in looking after his equipment properly. Whenever you bat, whether in a match or at a net, always wear pads, and gloves and a protector if you have them: not only can they save you from injury but they will give you confidence. Keep your pads clean and see that the straps are not so long as to flap beyond the buckles. If your cricket boots or shoes are leather-soled, see that they are properly nailed and be sure to keep the nails clear of mud. It is impossible to bowl or field well unless you are properly shod: a slip may cost you your wicket when batting, or mean missing a catch that can lose the match.

In choosing a bat be sure you can wield it easily: you cannot bat properly if your bat is too big or too heavy for you. You can test its "drive" by knocking up a ball with it. Do not think that only "white" blades are good. Look after your bat most carefully. If it is new, play it in by constantly knocking up an old ball with it. Keep the face clean with sandpaper: oil it when new, but once it is driving well a rub over once a week or so with an oily rag is all that it will need. Never let it get wet, e.g., from lying on wet grass. Never store it near a hot pipe or radiator in the winter. Never play with a loose rubber handle: get it stuck down again at once.

Take care of your cricket ball. Keep it clear of mud, especially the seam. If it gets wet never dry it in front of the fire: Dubbin or a colourless furniture cream will keep the leather in good condition.

THE MEANING OF LENGTH

There is an old saying that a virtue is always the mean between two extremes. The good length ball certainly lies between the extremes of the full-pitch and the long-hop, but to define it more accurately is no easy matter.

The real test of a good length ball is that it should present the batsman with a problem; the problem of deciding whether he should play forward or back to it. This means that it must not be so far up that he can really command it by a properly played forward stroke, or so short that he can watch it comfortably off the pitch when he plays back. But the area within which the ball can drop and present this problem cannot be laid down mathematically: it will vary according to a bowler's pace and the pace of the pitch, and even according to the batsman's build and reach.

The faster the bowler and the faster the pitch, the bigger is the margin within which a ball can be reckoned a good length. The slower the bowler and the slower the pitch, the smaller must that margin be. The margin for a really fast bowler on a fast pitch can be as much as 9 ft., whilst for a slow bowler on a dead wicket it can be little more than 3 ft.

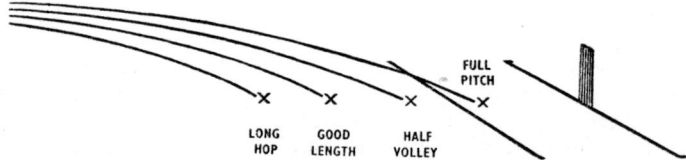

This diagram shows, in relation to each other, the terms given to balls of different lengths. The text explains how they can vary relative to batsman, bowler, and state of pitch.

A full pitch is one which the batsman can hit from the crease before it pitches.

A half-volley is one which, again from the crease, he can hit just after it has pitched.

A good length ball is one which sets the batsman a problem: whether to play back or forward to it.

The long hop is a ball which is so short that the batsman can watch it easily off the pitch, and force it for runs.

But length is also to some extent relative to the batsman; the taller the batsman and the more he really uses his reach in playing forward, the more he can reduce the "upper" limit of the bowler's margin of length; to a short batsman, or to one who relies chiefly on back play, the bowler will be able to pitch the ball further up.

His length may even be dictated to some extent by the state of the game. At one time he may be justified, even required, to tempt the batsman by keeping the ball right up, even to half-volley length. At another he may have to bowl "tight," i.e., just short of his normal length, in order to pin the batsman down to playing mainly off the back foot.

But as a general rule the young bowler's aim should always be to make the batsman play forward and this should be for him the test of his length. There are two reasons for this; the first is that there is always the chance of his making the ball "do" enough after it pitches to miss or edge the bat; the second is that, the fuller his length, the more "room" there must be in the air for the ball to swerve.

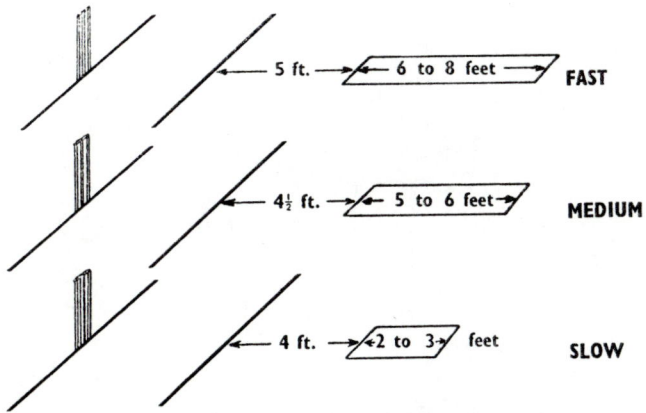

The above diagrams suggest the approximate target areas of "good length" for bowlers of different pace on a normal pitch.

So much for length from the bowler's point of view. What of the batsman's? His first object is to find the answer to this problem of length which the bowler is always trying to set him. He cannot hope to do so unless he makes proper use of his feet.

The further he moves his front foot in playing forward, provided he keeps his general balance and control, the more he can hope really to command the pitch of the ball. The further he moves his right foot back in playing back, the longer time will he have to watch the ball after it pitches. In playing good slow bowling, especially on a difficult wicket when the ball is really turning, the use of the feet in getting out to the pitch of the ball or even to meet it on the full pitch, is the hall-mark of good batsmanship.

The better a batsman can use his feet, the more he can reduce the bowler's margin of length, the more, in fact, can he make the bowler bowl where he, the batsman, wants, and the more difficult he will make it for him to bowl where he would like.

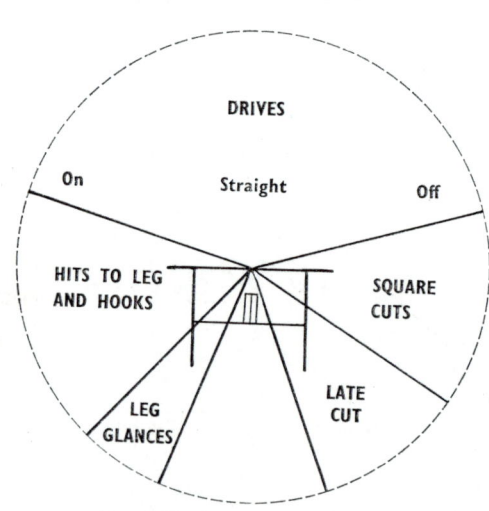

This diagram shows approximately the different directions of hits.

BATTING

To play any stroke successfully, the batsman must do three things: he must look at, "find", and then continue to watch the ball: he must decide what is the right stroke to play to it: he must make his body play that stroke correctly.

The first sounds easy enough, but in fact it is not. It is easy to think you are looking at the ball: it is fairly easy really to look at any given ball, provided you set your mind to it; but to build up the habit of watching, really watching, every ball throughout an innings means very hard work. You can only do it by learning to concentrate your mind and will on the job in hand. It is really a challenge to character, but if you can learn to meet it, it will stand you in good stead not only in cricket but in life.

To decide correctly what stroke to play to any particular ball is partly a matter of instinct, or what in cricket is often called "ball sense"; but it is mainly a matter of experience. In batting, as in everything else, some learn more quickly than others; but the more you think about the game, the more you try to analyse your own batting experience, the strokes that went right and those that went wrong, the sooner will you build up the judgment that will instinctively tell you how to deal with each successive ball.

The third element of batting is purely physical, the production of the right stroke in the right way. Now this too means hard work, for it means training your body to make a number of movements which are not natural, especially in what is really the basis of all good batting—learning to play straight—for the natural movement of the body is forwards and "fullchested", while to play straight it must move sideways and keep sideways. Again, in hitting at anything with two hands it is natural for the right, or lower hand, to do nearly all the work, but in all straight bat strokes the left, or top hand must be in control.

If then you really mean to become a batsman, you must first learn what you want to make your body do to play any particular stroke, and then, by going on playing it, groove your body into the movement so that what was at first unnatural and difficult becomes natural and automatic.

If you really study the analysis of the different strokes which follows, you will come to understand how you should play each of them. Once you understand that, practice is everything. You can do a great deal, even with one friend and at short range with a rubber ball, to "groove" any stroke. You can even, if you are keen enough, do much by yourself and without a ball; you can practise swinging the bat with the left hand only, for the more you can strengthen your left hand in this and every other possible way, the more power you will develop in it to control all straight bat strokes. You can also, of course, practise the different strokes without a ball, but in doing so be sure to play them each time to an imaginary ball and to "watch it all the way." Practice before a mirror will also help.

Finally, never forget that in all stroke play the position and steadiness of the head is vital; if your head moves into and stays in the right position, half the battle is won.

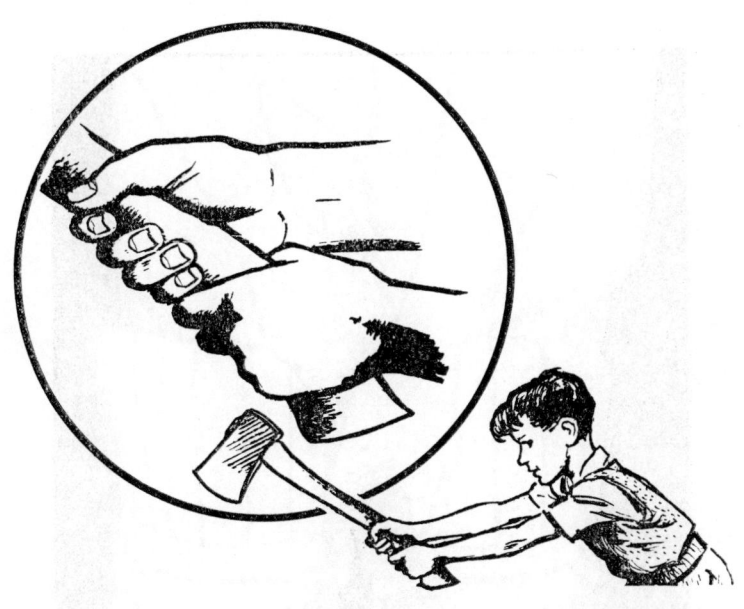

THE GRIP

This is a picture of hands gripping an axe. The grip of a bat is the same: natural, comfortable and powerful. Fingers and thumbs of both hands well round the handle; hands touching or very close together, with the right hand a little more than half way down the handle. The V's formed by thumb and forefinger should be in line with each other. The back of the left hand, if the bat is held upright, should face between mid-off and extra-cover.

THE GRIP

Fingers and thumbs well round handle. The V's formed by thumb and forefinger in line with each other.

THE GRIP

Left hand resting comfortably against left thigh. Hands close together.

THE STANCE

A comfortable, relaxed and balanced stance is most important. On it depends the true watching of the ball and the movement of the feet for every stroke. The feet should be roughly parallel, one on each side of the crease, some 4in. to 6in. apart, with toes pointing more or less towards point.

THE STANCE

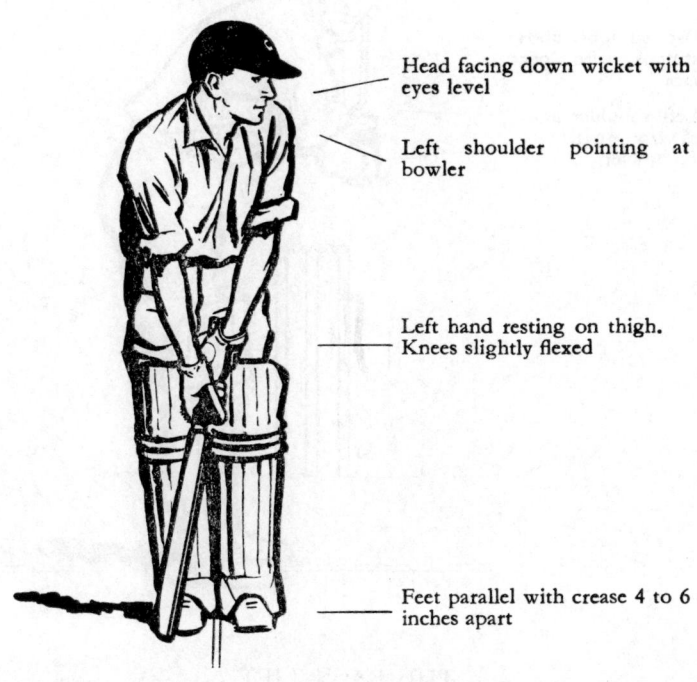

Head facing down wicket with eyes level

Left shoulder pointing at bowler

Left hand resting on thigh. Knees slightly flexed

Feet parallel with crease 4 to 6 inches apart

The weight should be evenly balanced and the knees slightly relaxed for easy and quick movement.

The left shoulder should point at the bowler with the body facing square to point. The head should be upright and turned full on the bowler with the eyes as level as possible. The left hand can rest comfortably against the left thigh.

As you wait for the ball, keep as still as possible. Be vigilant but relaxed.

THE BACK LIFT

Bat straight above stumps with open face

Left shoulder and elbow point to bowler

THE BACK LIFT

A correct back lift is of great importance. The left arm and wrist should do nearly all the work, the face of the bat opening naturally towards point as the bat lifts.

The head and body should be kept quite still. At the top of the lift, the right elbow should be slightly away from the body, and the left hand just opposite and above the right trouser pocket.

The bat should start its downward swing directly on the line of the intended stroke.

In attack, the back lift will naturally tend to be higher.

THE BACK LIFT

- Both eyes on bowler
- Head and body balanced and still
- Right elbow clear of body

Practise this back lift in front of a mirror. By getting it right, you will have gone a long way towards learning to keep a straight bat. In fact you can practise any stroke in this way.

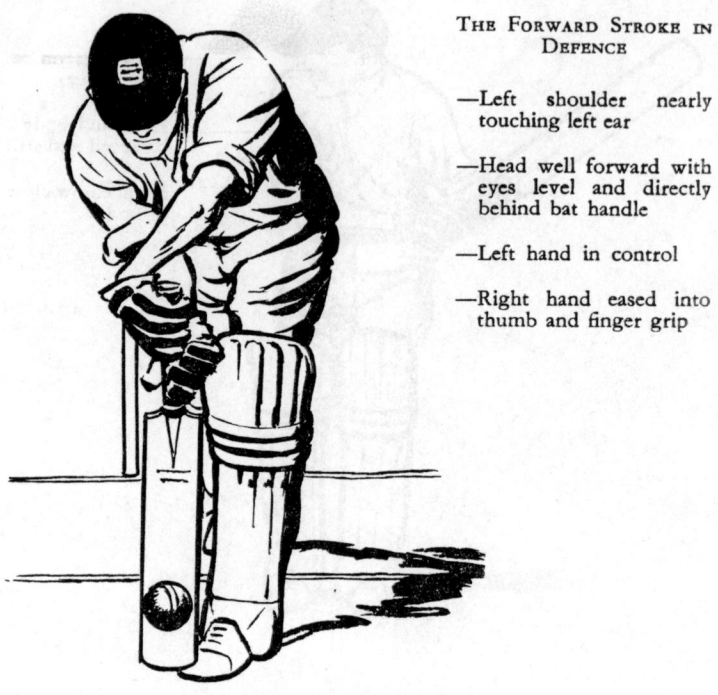

THE FORWARD STROKE IN DEFENCE

—Left shoulder nearly touching left ear

—Head well forward with eyes level and directly behind bat handle

—Left hand in control

—Right hand eased into thumb and finger grip

FORWARD DEFENSIVE STROKE TO A STRAIGHT BALL

The forward stroke is not only invaluable in defence, but the basis of all the drives. Learn to play it correctly and you are more than half way to becoming a batsman. The object is to play the ball as near as possible to the point where it pitches.

Lead with the head, left hip and shoulder out on to the line of the ball and aim to meet it with the bat a few inches in front of the left foot which should be pointing between mid-off and extra cover. The weight should be right forward over a bent

THE FORWARD STROKES

The Forward Stroke in Defence

| Right foot eased on to toe | Left knee bent | Ball met just in front of left toe and under line of eyes |

left knee. For this the right foot will naturally ease up, and when the ball is met, only the toe will be on the ground.

The left hand and wrist must control the stroke, the right hand relaxing into a thumb and finger grip. The longer the left hand keeps the full face of the blade moving down the line of the ball, the safer the stroke.

The head should be behind the top of the bat handle and over the point of contact, with the eyes watching the ball as long as possible.

THE FORWARD STROKE TO THE OFF-BALL

In general the stroke is the same as that for the straight ball, but the wider the ball, the more must the back of the left shoulder and hip be turned on the bowler and the wider should the left foot be pointed as it comes down just inside the line of the ball. The left knee will bend rather more than in playing the straight ball to ensure that "the gate is shut". The head will again lead the stroke, with the face kept as fully turned down the wicket as possible.

The batsman should never play the defensive forward stroke to any ball so wide that it does not threaten his wicket.

THE FORWARD STROKE TO THE ON-BALL

For balls well pitched up on or near the line of the leg stump the first movement should be a slight dipping of the left shoulder. This will help the batsman to lead out and over on to the line with his head and shoulder, with the left foot landing just outside the line of the ball with the toe pointing almost straight.

PRACTISING THE FORWARD STROKE

THE FORWARD STROKES

The straighter the ball the straighter must the stroke be aimed.

Keep the full face of the bat moving through as long as possible; beware of the right hand taking charge and of the left hip falling away. Either of these faults will make you play across the ball.

There is no better test of a young batsman than his ability to play this stroke securely.

PRACTISING THE FORWARD STROKES

Four of you can practise these strokes very effectively in a gymnasium or on an asphalt playground. Draw a target in chalk 6in. deep and 20in. across. The batsman takes his stance in such a position that this target is just where, depending on his reach, he can command the ball as it pitches.

The "bowler," standing some 7 to 8 yards away, lobs the ball on to the target. The other two stand at short mid-off and short mid-on. Straight balls should be played straight back, others on the appropriate line. Three or four minutes each, and change round. Criticise each other's style.

FROM WICKET TO BOWLER—7 TO 8 YARDS

—Left shoulder well round on bowler
—Head facing down wicket
—Left arm in strong control
—Bat face has opened

THE START OF THE STRAIGHT DRIVE

THE DRIVES

The drive is the most exhilarating stroke in cricket and an invaluable weapon in any batsman's armoury of attack. As he matures in physique and experience, every young batsman should begin to feel that the half-volley is a challenge which he is ready and eager to meet. To be able to do so may make all the difference to his ability to dictate to the bowler and to force a more defensive disposition of the field.

The Drive Impact

—Left arm still controlling the arc of the swing

—Right foot eased to allow weight to come forward

—Ball met close to left foot and immediately below eyes

The technique of the drives, whether straight, on or off, is really the same as that for the forward strokes, except that the bat lift is higher and the ball is hit just beside the left toe rather than met in front of it.

The power of the drive comes from a lengthened and accelerated swing in which arms, wrists and hands all take part. The arc of this swing must be as long, smooth and flat as possible; the left arm and hand must control it; the right hand will reinforce and accelerate it just before the bat meets the ball, but it must not come in too early or it will tend to pull the swing across the line of the ball.

A good principle to aim at in driving is to keep the left arm as close as possible to the body in the back swing and the right arm as close as possible to it in the forward swing.

As in the forward stroke, lead with your head, left shoulder and hip on to the line of the ball.

THE FOLLOW-THROUGH

—Head leading

—Weight full on the front foot and leaning into line of stroke

Watch the ball all the way: to do so you must keep balanced and keep your head as level as you can. Resist the temptation to lift your head.

Control in driving is essential; if you try to hit too hard, your drive may well become a dig or a heave instead of a swing.

Think in terms of hitting the ball smoothly and cleanly past the in-fields rather than of carrying the boundary.

Provided the ball is far enough up, the drive can be played with a single stride, but you must also learn to "use your feet" to get to the pitch of the slower, higher and shorter ball. To do

The Follow-Through

—Head has been kept level

—Arms have swung well through in the direction the ball has been hit

—Left toe pointing to mid-off

this you must learn to glide out, with your right foot moving up behind your left until the final stride. Only so can you keep sideways with your left shoulder to the line. Make this glide as smooth and as flat as you can and be sure that your head leads.

This ability to use your feet to get to the pitch of the ball is invaluable in playing slow bowling; go all the way; it is far better to be stumped by a yard than by six inches. But remember that, the wider the ball is on the off-side, the more difficult it is to move both out and across to it. A slow bowler who knows his business will try to tempt a good driver to chase the wide flighted ball.

MOVING OUT TO DRIVE

1.

—Weight moving forward on to left foot

—High bat lift

—Left shoulder pointing at bowler

2.

Head steady and on line of ball—

Back of left shoulder turned on bowler
Left arm in control—

Right foot gliding up behind and just past left heel, thus keeping body sideways—

MOVING OUT TO DRIVE

MOVING OUT TO DRIVE (*continued*)

. (*continued*)

at face open —

Head and
ft shoulder
ading—

eft foot about to move
nto final stride—

3. Head has been kept steady—

Arms have swung well through in the direction the ball has gone—

Left toe pointing to mid-off

FINISH OF THE OFF-DRIVE

Hands have finished high in the direction the ball has gone—

Head and body leaning into the stroke—

Left foot has been taken over to just inside line of ball with toe facing extra cover—

THE OFF-DRIVE

The most important thing in off-driving is to get your head, left shoulder and hip over on to the line of the ball; if they are right, the left foot will look after itself. The wider the ball, the more should the back of the left shoulder be turned on the bowler and the wider on the off-side should the stroke be aimed. The bat will in fact start its downward swing from the line of fine leg. Keep the full face of the bat moving through the line of the stroke as long as possible.

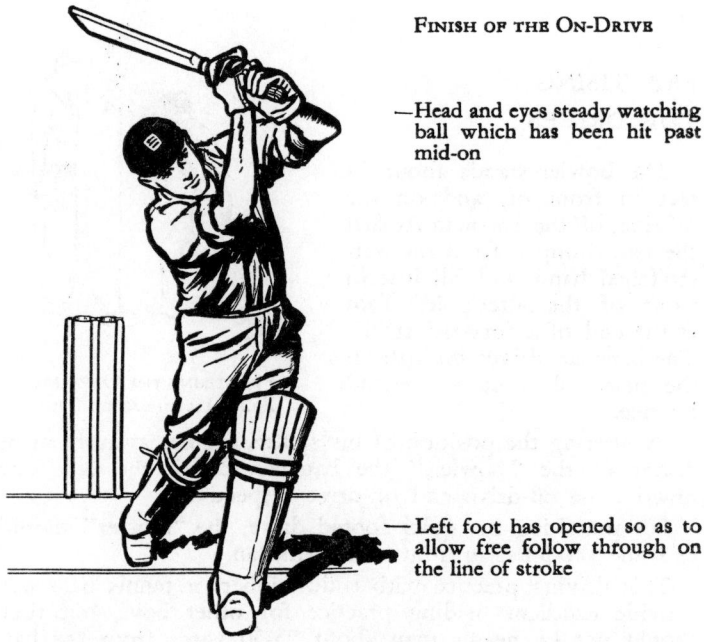

FINISH OF THE ON-DRIVE

—Head and eyes steady watching ball which has been hit past mid-on

—Left foot has opened so as to allow free follow through on the line of stroke

THE ON-DRIVE

The ability to on-drive is rare with boys, but if they can acquire it they will greatly increase their scoring power.

The first movement is a slight dipping of the left shoulder; this will allow the left foot and the line of balance, with the head leading, to come out on to the line of the ball; the left foot will land just outside that line.

The straighter the ball, the straighter must the stroke be aimed and the longer will the full face of the bat be moving down the line. The batsman must strongly resist the tendency to "pull" his on-drives by allowing the right hand and right shoulder to play too big a part; he must not allow his left hip to fall away.

PRACTISING THE DRIVES

The bowler stands about 2½ feet in front of, and on the off-side, of the batsman so that the ball dropped from his outstretched hand will fall just in front of the latter's left foot at the end of a forward stride. The batsman drives the ball on the half volley of its second bounce.

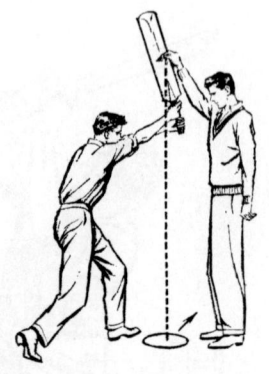

PRACTISING THE OFF-DRIVE
Ball is hit on second bounce

By altering the position of his stance, further away from or nearer to the "bowler," the batsman can in the same way practise the off-drive and on-drive respectively.

For practising the quick-footed drive, the "bowler" should be some 4 to 5 feet in front of the batsman.

This driving practice with solid rubber or tennis balls can provide excellent fielding practice for other boys, but they should not be nearer than about 25-30 yards from the bat.

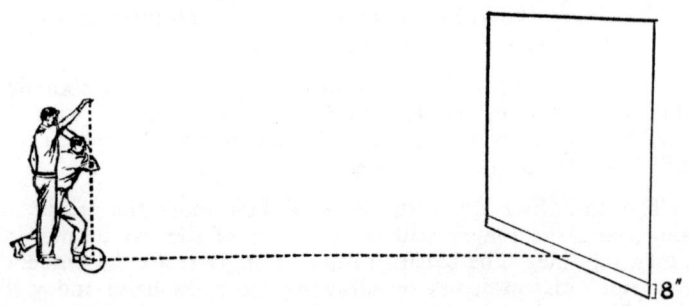

PRACTISING THE QUICK FOOTED DRIVE

PRACTISING THE DRIVES

Alternatively, it can be practised against a wall or net or quite safely at short range with plastic balls.

These practices can be of tremendous value and also the greatest fun, but it is essential that throughout them the batsman should concentrate on the "shape" and balance of his stroke as already outlined. Wild hitting will do more harm than good.

CLASS PRACTICE INTO TENNIS NET

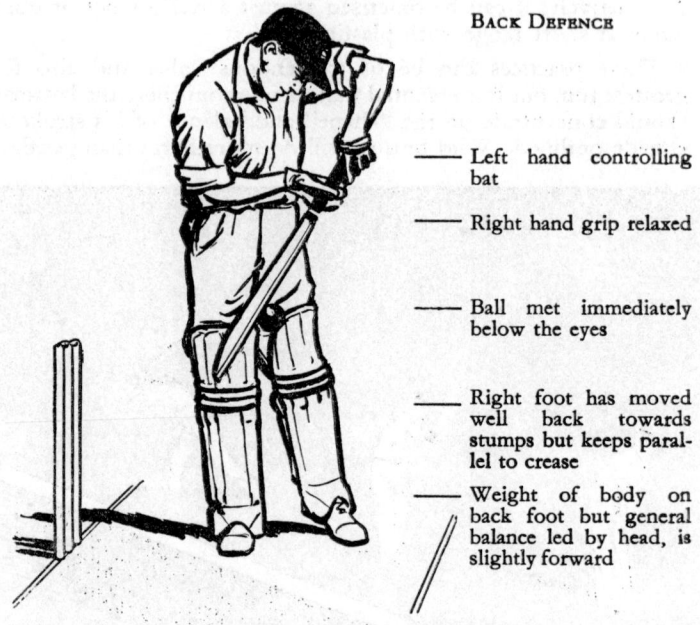

THE BACK STROKE IN DEFENCE

Unless a batsman can, by playing forward, command the pitch of the ball, he must play back and so have time to watch whatever it may do after pitching. The slower and more difficult the wicket, the more he must rely on back play.

The right foot moves well back and just inside the line of the ball with the toe pointing parallel to the crease. The weight is transferred on to this foot but the balance of the head remains slightly forward. The left foot, eased up on to the toe, acts as a balancer.

The ball should be met just below the eyes which should be as level as possible as they watch the ball down the pitch. The stroke is controlled by the left wrist and arm with the elbow high. The right hand relaxes into a thumb and finger grip. The body must be kept sideways as much as possible.

THE BACK STROKE IN DEFENCE

BACK DEFENCE

Head on line of ball with eyes level—

Left shoulder and elbow high—

Left hand controlling bat, right grip relaxed—

Right toe pointing just behind cover—

For an off ball the stroke is the same but the right foot moves further across and may point slightly behind point, and the back of the left shoulder is turned slightly on the bowler.

For a ball on, or just outside the leg stump, the right foot will point towards extra cover and the left shoulder will open slightly towards mid-on.

In every case the full face of the bat must be kept on the line of the ball.

THE ATTACKING BACK STROKE

Where the ball is short enough for the batsman to feel in real command, he can lengthen and quicken the swing of his back stroke to force it for runs.

The body must be kept sideways and the left arm must still control the stroke, but the right hand should reinforce it with a "punch" just before impact. There will be a strong follow-through in the direction in which the ball has gone.

Unless he is of fair height or has exceptional strength in forearms and wrists, this is not an easy stroke for a young batsman to command. In any case he must beware of trying to force the ball too hard, for in doing so he may move his head and dip his right shoulder which will probably mean that he will lift or edge the ball.

PRACTISING BACK STROKES

These can be practised at short range on the same lines as the forward strokes (see page 25). But the target will, of course, be drawn much shorter than for the forward stroke and the "bowler" will bowl or throw the ball at it rather faster, getting well down to do so in order that the ball shall not rise too abruptly. Again there will be fielders on the off and on side who will take their turn to bat.

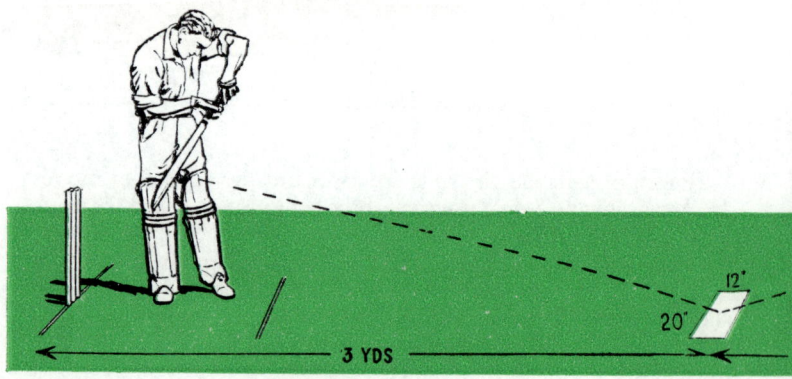

PRACTISING THE BACK STROKE

THE ATTACKING BACK STROKE

THE ATTACKING BACK STROKE TO AN OFF BALL

Full follow through —

Head leading into line of stroke —

Body sideways —

Left foot eased off heel
Right foot pointing parallel with crease —

◄— 4-5 YDS. —►

PRACTISING THE BACK STROKE

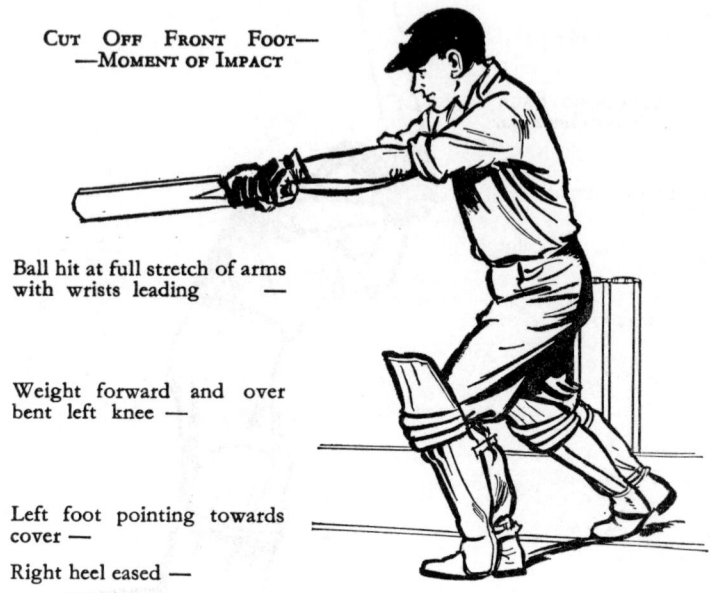

CUT OFF FRONT FOOT—
—MOMENT OF IMPACT

Ball hit at full stretch of arms with wrists leading —

Weight forward and over bent left knee —

Left foot pointing towards cover —

Right heel eased —

HORIZONTAL BAT STROKES

A boy will never become a batsman unless he learns to play straight, but he must also learn to punish the bad ball and this is often most effectively done by cross-bat strokes. This is particularly true of the long-hop and full-toss to leg which, especially in junior cricket, offer the best chances of hitting fours.

These strokes are much easier, because they are much more natural than the straight bat strokes, but to play them with certainty, you must learn to play them correctly.

The Cuts

Cutting is a very effective way of getting runs off short balls outside the off stump, especially from quick bowling. According to whether it is played early or late, the ball can be hit as square as cover or as fine as second slip. But for the cut to be

CUT OFF FRONT FOOT
—THE FINISH

— Head and body still leaning into the stroke

— The right wrist has "climbed" over the left to keep the ball down

made safely, the ball must be short enough for the batsman to watch it rise off the pitch, and wide enough to give him plenty of room for the stroke.

For all cuts, the bat must be picked well up and rather towards fine-leg, with the right elbow well clear of the body and the back of the left shoulder slightly turned on the bowler.

Cut off the Front Foot

This stroke is played to hit the really short and wide ball at the top of its rise just to the left or right of cover point. The back of the left shoulder is turned on the bowler, and the left foot moves well out and across to land pointing at extra cover. The wrists and hands then "throw" the bat down and out at the ball to meet it at the full stretch of the arms opposite the body.

The right wrist turns over the left to keep the ball down.

Cut Off Back Foot —Moment of Impact

— Head and weight into the stroke over right knee

— Ball met at full stretch of arms, just opposite right hip

— Right foot facing just behind point

Cut Off Back Foot —The Finish

Full follow-through —

Weight still leaning into stroke —

Square Cut off the Back Foot

The right foot moves across, to land facing point and the ball is met opposite to, or rather behind, the line of the right hip. Again the wrists and hands are thrown out and down, from a high bat lift, and the head and body follow into the line of the stroke over the bent right knee.

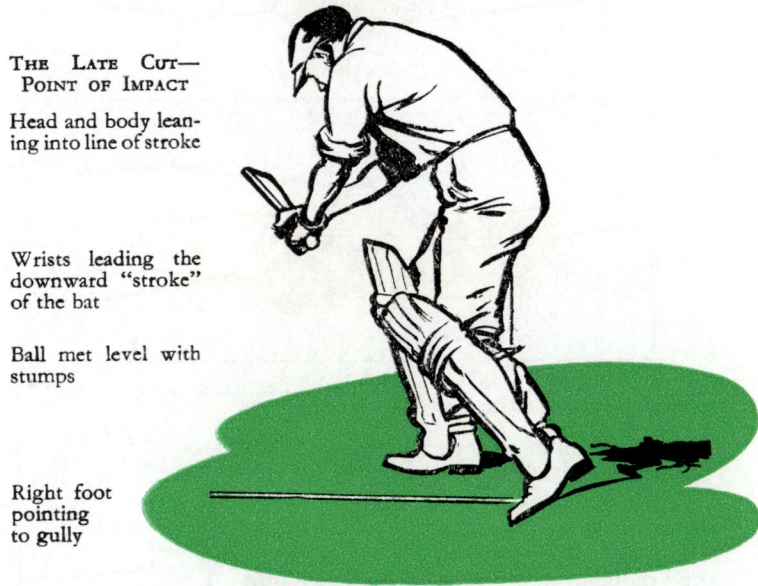

THE LATE CUT—
POINT OF IMPACT

Head and body leaning into line of stroke

Wrists leading the downward "stroke" of the bat

Ball met level with stumps

Right foot pointing to gully

The Late Cut

This stroke is the same as the above except that it starts with a more pronounced turn of the left shoulder, and the right foot lands further back and pointing to third slip. The ball is met later, nearly level with the stumps and, with wrists leading, the batsman "strokes" rather than hits it in the direction of gully or second slip.

In both these cuts, the left foot will ease up on to the toe to allow the weight to come fully over the bent right knee.

WRIST MOVEMENT

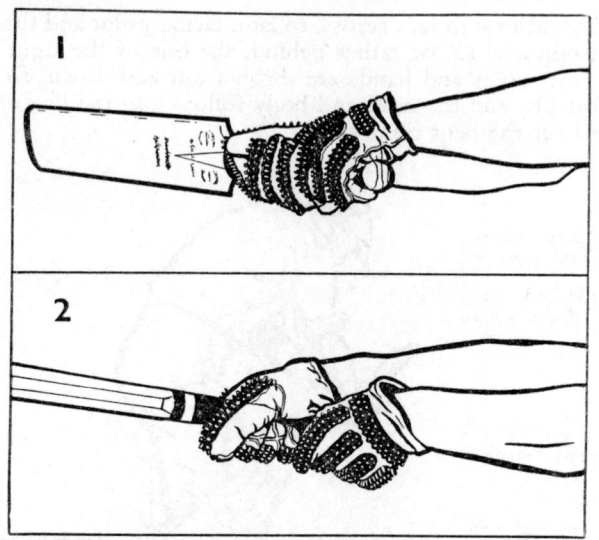

Wrist Action in the Cut

The action of the wrists in the cut is like that of a double-handed throw outwards and downwards. At the start both wrists are slightly "cocked"; at the moment of impact the "V's" of the hands are in the same line, but the right wrist is beginning to climb over the left wrist until it finishes with the back of that hand pointing upwards.

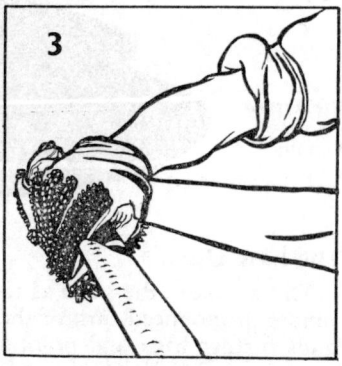

Hitting the Leg Ball

The ability to take full toll from full tosses and long hops to leg may well be, at least for a year or two for quite young batsmen, the most productive source of runs. To do so is much

HITTING THE FULL PITCH TO LEG

Head and weight forward on to left foot

Ball met at full stretch of arms

Left foot out on to line of ball

easier than to get runs with a straight bat, for it involves a basically natural cross-batted stroke played mainly with the bottom hand: but even so there is a right way to play it, and a determined effort to learn this will pay a big dividend.

The Full Pitch to Leg

The left leg should move well out and over on to the line of the ball; the head should lead the body well forward on to this line over the bent left knee. The ball will be met at the full stretch of the arms and hit mainly with the right hand.

The stroke should be aimed in front of square leg, though the wider the ball, the more will it inevitably tend to travel behind the wicket.

The main reason the young batsman so often misses or miss-hits the full pitch to leg is that he tries to hit too hard and so fails to look at the ball. He must keep balanced, keep his head still and, in making the stroke, think in terms of "quickness" and not of "effort".

HITTING THE LONG HOP TO LEG — JUST BEFORE IMPACT

Weight on right foot but balance forward with head directly on line of ball—

Ball met at full stretch of arms—

Right foot well back and just outside line of ball—

Right toe pointing down the pitch—

Left foot carried away to open up body—

Low full pitches on or near the leg stump should not be hit "cross-batted", but forced wide of mid-on with a straight bat.

The Long Hop to Leg

As in the back stroke, the right foot will move well back, but it will open up so that it lands pointing to extra cover or mid-off; the left foot will move back naturally after it and land pointing nearly straight down the wicket, so that the body is now almost fully open, with the head over on the line of the ball.

Though the feet move back, the balance of head and body must be well forward. The mechanism of the stroke will be the same as that already analysed for hitting the full pitch to leg, and there must be the same emphasis on body balance and on speed rather than on effort in hitting.

Hitting the Long Hop to Leg— Finish

—Ball has been hit just in front of square leg

—Weight has carried over on to the left foot

—Right wrist has turned over to keep the ball down

The most common reason these balls are so often miss-hit or missed is that the batsman hits too hard and too late and fails to look at the ball. Keep your balance forward; meet the ball well in front of you.

Practising Leg-Strokes

You can practise these strokes very easily by getting a friend to bowl you, at short range with a rubber ball, full pitches or long hops, and hitting them against a wall, or to two or three fielders stationed well away from you for whom it is also good fielding practice.

In this practice concentrate on really watching the ball and see how often you can hit it in front of, rather than behind, square leg.

START OF THE
HOOK STROKE

Head and balance slightly forward

Bat taken back outside line of ball

Body opening full

Right foot moving across so as to land just beyond line of ball, with toe pointing down wicket

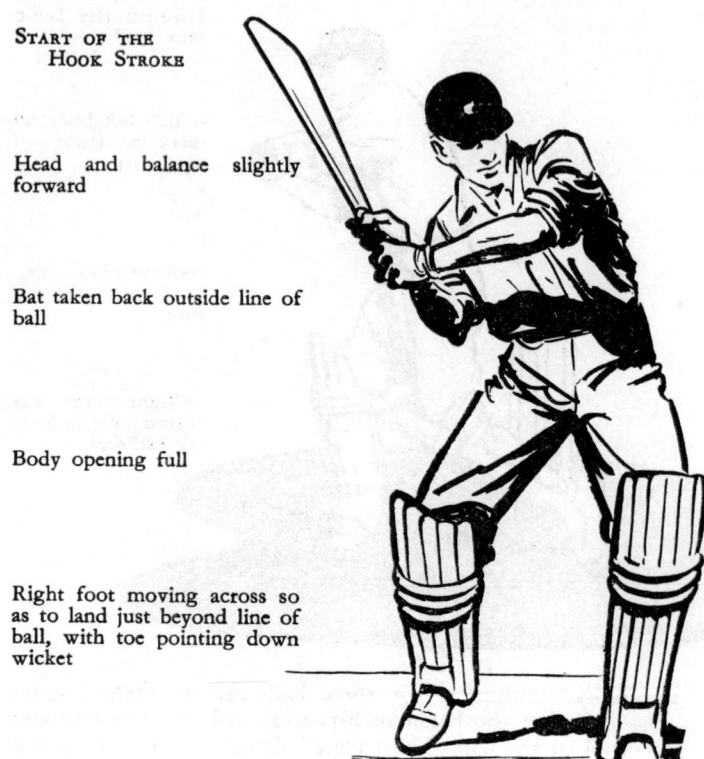

The Hook Stroke

The hook is the name commonly given to the stroke by which a short ball on the wicket, or even to the off-side of it, is hit round to the on-side with a cross bat.

Hook Stroke—The Finish

— Body has pivoted on right foot

— Head and body leaning in the direction of the stroke and perfectly balanced

— Right wrist has "climbed" over left to keep ball down

— Left foot has been carried back

To hook effectively, it is essential that the right foot should be carried so far across the wicket that the head and body are just outside the line of the ball. This really turns it into a short ball to leg which can be dealt with exactly as already described.

But the hook is a dangerous stroke for any but experienced players and most boys will be well-advised to use the much safer forcing back stroke with a straight bat.

THE LEG GLANCES

The ability to "deflect" the ball to leg will certainly bring a batsman runs, especially against fast bowling or medium paced bowling on fast wickets. But it must never be thought of as any substitute for playing the ball on the on-side with the full face of the bat, still less for hitting it to leg for four when it is possible to do so.

Whether played off the front or the back foot, the leg glance is played with a virtually straight bat; but just before it meets the ball the bat is moving slightly across the line, and the face of it is shutting. There is, therefore, no room for error and the stroke should never be played to a ball inside the line of the batsman's pads.

Leg Glance off the Front Foot

This is best played to a ball which is on or just outside the batsman's pads and just over a length but not far enough up to be driven. Until just before impact the stroke is the same as the forward stroke to an on-side ball, except that the left leg is brought just inside the ball's line.

The ball should be met almost under the eyes and just in front of the left leg, with the wrists turning the bat face slightly just before impact. The tendency of most young batsmen is to start closing the bat face too soon and so very often to miss it.

Leg Glance off the Back Foot

The ball, again on or just outside the batsman's pads, will in this case be just short of a length.

As in the back stroke, the right foot will move well back and far enough across to allow the left foot, also moving back and landing nearly level with it, to be just inside the line of the ball; the right foot will be pointing towards mid-off and the left almost straight down the wicket. The ball will be met only just in front of the left leg and approximately below the eyes.

In both the leg-glances the left hand should keep control of the bat as long as possible.

THE LEG GLANCES

Leg Glance off Front Foot

— Head forward over point of impact

— Left hand in control

— Blade of bat just beginning to shut

— Ball met just in front of left foot

Leg Glance off Back Foot
Head forward and over point of impact —
Right foot pointing down wicket —
Left foot just behind right heel —
Ball just in front of left knee —

RUNNING BETWEEN THE WICKETS

Good running between the wickets is very important. It can bring batsmen many runs, sometimes even enough to decide the result of a match. It can unsettle the bowlers and fielders. Judgment, based on experience, is the first essential, but there are some principles which should always be followed.

CALLING

(a) Except when the ball goes behind the wicket, the striker must always call. The non-striker must always call when it does.

(b) The call should be "YES", "NO", or "WAIT" and must be quick, clear and firm. A call can always be reinforced by saying "Probably two" or "Probably three" as you pass your partner, but not so loud as to stimulate the fielders. If a call is refused, it must be refused at once and firmly with "NO".

(c) Once both batsmen are really committed to a run, they should always go through with it.

(d) Never call for a misfield, unless you are sure that the ball is right past the fielder and beyond quick recovery.

RUNNING

(a) The non-striker should stand well wide of the return crease on the opposite side of the wicket from that where the bowler is bowling. He should always keep to that side for the run, just as the striker should keep to the bowler's side. When the bowling is round the wicket, the non-striker should stand really wide so as to be sure of being clear of the striker in his normal running ground.

(b) The non-striker should hold his bat in his left hand (right hand if the bowling is round the wicket) and, as the bowler delivers the ball, should start moving down the wicket ready for instant acceleration into a run if called. He must always be ready to change the bat from one hand to the other during a run so that, as he reaches the crease for the turn, he will be looking to where the ball has been hit.

(c) Always slide the bat along the ground at the full stretch of your arm for the last two yards or so of your run.

(d) Never look behind you during a run to see if there is a second or a third. Complete the run as fast as you can, turn, look and call.

PLAYING AN INNINGS

It is one thing to be able to play strokes whether in attack or defence, but it is quite another thing to play an innings. To do so demands an alert mind, cool judgment, and often a stout heart. Above all it needs the self-control that will not be upset by early difficulties or by getting away to a flying start.

Here are some points which the young batsmen should always try to remember. Accept cheerfully whatever place in the order your captain allots you. Get padded-up and be ready to go in with plenty of time in hand. Before you go in accustom yourself to the light in which you will have to bat. As you watch the game, take stock of the bowlers and try to see what they are doing with the ball and their general methods of attack, so that, when you go in, you may have some idea of what you are up against, but however well they seem to be bowling, don't let this get you down, and however badly, don't imagine that it is a case of "help yourself". Watch, too, how the field is placed and try to pick out the fielders with whom it would be dangerous to take any sort of risk and those who are slow of foot or who have to wind-up to throw, for they may well offer you some extra runs.

As you go out to the wicket, remind yourself that the most important thing of all in batting is to watch the ball, every ball; for batting consists in playing one ball at a time on its merits whatever has happened to the one before, whether it has nearly bowled you or you have hit it for a brilliant four. Keep reminding yourself of this all the way through your innings. Also, that leading with your head and keeping your balance are vital to all proper stroke play. Nothing is more infuriating than losing your wicket to a thoroughly bad ball through a wild unbalanced stroke. Don't worry about "breaking your duck". If the bowling is accurate, be content to stay in and get a sight of the ball and to become accustomed to the light and the pace of the wicket. Once you are set, the runs will come; the bowlers will get tired before you do. Have a good look at each new bowler and don't assume that you can always go on with him where you left off with the others.

Remember always that you have a partner at the other end: be as much of a partner to him as you can. Run his runs as fast as, even faster than, your own. The right word at the right time may do a lot to encourage him if he is in trouble, or steady him if he is getting wild.

Always be on the lookout for a quick single. It unsettles the bowlers and may rattle the field. But no run is ever worth the risk of a wicket.

Always "play to the score" and to your captain's wishes, even if it may mean risking the sacrifice of your wicket. But remember that in chasing runs against the clock, a good start means much. A side can always press on later, if they have wickets "in the bank".

After every innings that you play, think back and see what lessons can be learnt for the next. Never let failure get you down. All the greatest batsmen have known it. Keep fighting and the tide will turn.

NET PRACTICE

Unless it is taken really seriously, net practice can do more harm than good. Careless, slap-dash batting and bowling at a net can easily lead to disaster in a match.

Whether in batting or bowling the young cricketer must try his hardest all the time; the harder he tries, the more value he will get from his net and the more, in fact, he will enjoy it.

Four is the ideal number for a net, a batsman and three bowlers. If there has to be more, the bowlers should take it in turn to rest or to field out.

The pitch must be as good as possible and boys should always be ready to help roll it before a net and between batsmen's innings, if it gets cut up.

The bowler's crease should always be properly marked out.

All pads, gloves, etc. should be well behind or to the side of a net so that each batsman can pad up in safety.

No bowler must ever turn his back on the batsman at the net when another one is bowling.

The Batsman

He must always wear pads and gloves, and a protector if he has one, for net practice. He should be sure to take a proper guard.

Throughout his innings the batsman should wait until all his bowlers have bowled before returning the balls to them: this should be done by lobbing an easy catch and never by casually hitting the ball up the net with his bat.

For the first few minutes of his net he should concentrate on playing himself in, just as he would in a match, getting the pace of the wicket and sizing up the various bowlers opposed to him. He must try consciously in every net to build up this habit of really watching the ball.

After this first spell of "settling-in" he may ask the bowlers —and the coach if there is one present—to help him to try to improve some particular element in his batting, especially in attacking stroke play, e.g., the drives or in hitting the long-hop or the full pitch to leg. If he really improves the technique of even one stroke in any net innings, he will have achieved much.

For the last spell of his innings he may ask the coach or bowlers to set him a target of runs and then get down to a real battle with them to reach it. He must ask each bowler at the start to tell him how his field is set and perhaps ask them to bowl in overs rather than one after another.

If there is a coach at the net he will assess the run value of any given stroke and also the fate of any possible chance. If there is not, this will probably be a matter of considerable, if friendly, argument. But after all, nothing very vital is at stake!

The Bowler

He should take this net practice just as seriously as the batsman. He should always take his proper run and make up his mind before each ball what he is trying to do. Net practice is the time when he can build up his concentration and control with the comforting knowledge that he will not be taken off!

He is justified at a net in experimenting with spin, swerve and change of pace rather more than he would in a match, but he should never do so at the expense of his normal run up and his proper basic action. Bowlers must never forget that their full co-operation is essential, if the batsmen are to get full value from the net. At times they may be asked to give a batsman practice in some particular stroke and this can be a valuable test of their control of length and direction. Though naturally concentrating on their own job of bowling, they should listen to all that the coach may have to say to the batsman and store it up in their own minds against the time when it is their turn to bat. A bowler should never go on bowling at a net if he begins to feel tired. He should ask to have a rest—and put on his sweater.

BOWLING

THE BASIC ACTION

Most boys, if only they have enough determination and will really get down to consistent and intelligent practice, can learn to bowl well enough to enjoy it and to be of some value to their side. How each boy will bowl best will depend upon a number of factors such as his general physique, the strength and length of his fingers, his temperament, and so on. It will naturally be a matter for experiment, of trial and error, but the sooner he can make up his mind about it the better, and once he has made it up, he must stick to it and try to make the very best of himself on the line he has chosen.

The first requirement for all bowlers is control of length and direction; without it the other bowling virtues of pace, spin and flight lose much of their value. The secret of this control for all bowlers lies in determination and in acquiring a good basic action. For whatever may be the difference in their individual methods there are certain basic principles which every bowler should try to observe. They are:

(1) The Grip

The ball must never be held in the palm of the hand but always near the end of the fingers. It is the "whip" of the wrist and the fingers that adds life to the ball and helps to give it pace off the pitch. The variation of grip for the different breaks and the swerve will be described later.

(2) The Run-Up

The object of a run-up is simply to bring the bowler to the crease completely balanced, with the rhythm and momentum necessary to bowl and to go on bowling his "stock" ball.

The young bowler must experiment for himself to decide what is the minimum length of run necessary to achieve this; once found, he must stick to it so that his run-up may become automatic.

This approach to the wicket must build up gradually and naturally; it should be smooth and relaxed, with the balance of the body slightly forward and the head kept steady.

As he starts his run-up, the bowler should have a clear picture in his mind of the particular ball he wants to bowl and as he approaches the wicket he should concentrate his mind and his eyes on the spot where he means to drop it.

Young bowlers cannot take too much trouble to get their run right, for it is the essential preliminary to:

(3) The Delivery

The essence of a good action is that the body, with the arm as its extension, should wind up like a spring and then unwind in the actual delivery of the ball and in the follow-through. In this action there are four vital phases:

(a) *The last but one stride of the run-up* is more or less a jump off the left foot with the body turning sideways, and the right foot passing in front of the left, the right hand is now close to the face and the left arm is beginning to stretch upwards.

(b) *The beginning of the delivery stride:*

The front foot lands parallel to the bowling crease and the body completes the turning movement so that the left shoulder is pointing towards the batsman; the weight is on the right foot and the body is leaning slightly away from the batsman with the back a little arched. The left arm is extended upwards and the head, steady and not leaning away, is looking down the wicket from behind it. The spring is now "cocked" and ready for release in:

(c) *The completion of the delivery stride:*

The left shoulder, hip and leg lead the forward swing of the body, with the left arm thrown out towards the batsman and acting as a rudder, the right arm swinging up.

The left foot lands flat, in line with the right, and pointing to long leg. The length of this stride must depend on the bowler's physical make-up.

He must try to keep sideways as long as possible, i.e., until just before his left foot lands; he must keep his head as still as he can and not allow it to fall back or dip forward. At the moment of delivery his left side should be as braced as possible with his weight full on his front foot.

His bowling arm, with the wrist "whipping" through, should be as high as possible.

(*d*) *The follow-through:*

As the right arm comes through after delivering the ball the body continues to pivot until the right shoulder is pointing to the batsman. By this time the right arm has carried across in front of the left thigh and the left arm has swung back close to the body until it is well up and clear from it.

The follow-through will be continued for several strides and should be as straight as is consistent with not cutting up the playing area of the pitch with spikes.

REMEMBER TO AIM FOR

(1) **Concentration of the mind and will on the intended ball.**

(2) **A consistent, smooth and balanced run up.**

(3) **Correct start of the delivery stride, with the front foot parallel to the bowling crease, the left arm high, and the head looking down the wicket from behind that arm.**

(4) **Keeping sideways as long as possible.**

(5) **Not delivering the ball until the full weight is on the front foot.**

(6) **Making the most of your height, i.e., keeping the bowling arm high and not letting the left leg and side "crumple."**

(7) **Keeping the head steady throughout.**

(8) **A full and lively follow-through.**

THE SPRING OFF THE LEFT FOOT

Body turning sideways
Right hand near face
Left hand stretching up
Head upright and looking full down wicket

THE BEGINNING OF THE DELIVERY STRIDE

Front foot parallel to bowling crease
Left shoulder pointing at batsman
Left arm stretching well up
Back slightly arched
Head steady and looking down wicket from behind left arm
Right arm beginning the delivery swing

THE DELIVERY STRIDE

Left foot has landed in line with the right foot and is pointing to mid off

Left side braced

Right arm high

Left arm close to side

THE FOLLOW-THROUGH

Pivot of the body has brought right shoulder through to point at batsman

Right arm has carried down and across left thigh

Left arm has swung well up and back

Head still balanced and leading down line of delivery

Learning to Bowl (1)

Beginners can learn the basic actions by standing with feet astride and arms sideways as shown above. First rock from one foot to the other, keeping arms stretched out sideways.

Practising Length and Direction

Remember the main points in the basic action as you bowl and concentrate your mind and eyes on the target.

LEARNING TO BOWL (II)

Next, continue the same rocking action but with arms swinging loosely in cartwheel fashion into the bowling position, as above. Be sure to look at the batsman over your left shoulder. Now do this with a ball and after rocking a few times, let the ball go. Keep looking at the spot where you want the ball to pitch.

SPIN BOWLING

Spin bowlers are of two types, off-spinners and leg-spinners; the latter also hope to command the googly.

It is much easier to combine accuracy of length and direction with some off-spin than with leg-spin, but on good wickets it is easier to make the ball really spin from leg than from off. In school cricket particularly a leg-spinner is invaluable, provided that he can combine his spin with reasonable accuracy; but to do so needs much determination and practice.

Only by experiment and practice can a young bowler make up his mind whether he means to become a spin bowler. He should then decide which spin he wants to bowl and stick to it. He should *not* try to combine off-spinners with leg-spinners or he may fall between two stools, besides setting his captain an insoluble problem over his field placing.

The first stage in this experiment is to learn how to really spin the ball; this means mastering the correct grips and the right use of the fingers and wrist to provide "leverage."

The Off Break

The lever of the spin is the inside of the top joint of the first finger, pressed hard against the seam. The wider the space between the first and second fingers, as they grip the ball, the greater will be the leverage. To secure maximum turn of the ball, the wrist must be cocked back and, as the ball is bowled, should turn outwards and forwards in a movement like that of turning a door knob from left to right.

To help both spin and flight, the body should be kept sideways as long as possible: the ball should be bowled across the body and delivered just as the arm is passing the head. At the finish of the delivery swing, the palm of the hand will be pointing upwards.

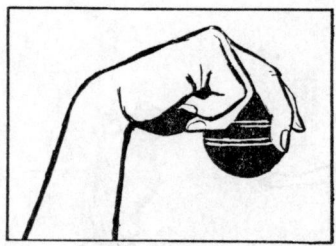 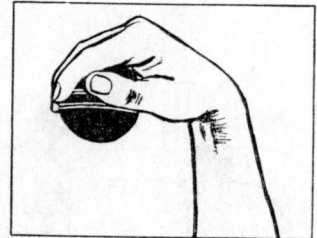

THE GRIP FOR LEG BREAK

(a) Viewed from behind bowler   (b) Viewed by batsman

The Leg Break

The lever of the spin is the inside of the top joint of the bent third finger flying along the seam and pressing hard against it. The first two fingers, naturally spaced, lie across the seam. The wrist is cocked inward and flips straight as the ball is delivered in an action similar to turning a door knob from right to left: at the same time the third finger is flicked outward toward the batsman and thumb downward away from him.

The palm of the hand must be kept facing the batsman for as long as possible: if turned over too soon, top spin or a googly will result, and these, though valuable, are no substitute for the leg break. After delivery the hand will finish with the palm pointing downward.

The Googly

The grip is the same as for the leg break. But the hand turns over earlier so that at the moment of delivery its back is turned on the batsman and the ball comes out over the top of the third and little finger. To do this the bowler will have to open up his action, dipping his left shoulder slightly and making his left foot land with toe pointing straight down the wicket and not at fine leg.

LEARNING TO BOWL THE LEG BREAK IN THREE STAGES
Learn one thoroughly before trying the next

Learning to Spin

First, master the grips; then practise in pairs at quite short range. The leg break can best be learnt by bowling underarm and preferably with a solid rubber ball and on a surface that will take spin. The off break can best be learnt at the very outset by means of the throwing action.

Then, still at short range, practise bowling round arm and gradually raise the arm until you can bowl your spin overarm, taking care to make your body pivot properly as described in the basic action.

Then begin to extend the range at which you are bowling and preface the action with a run-up, until you are bowling at full range and with your full normal run-up.

Remember that in spin, as in stock, bowling rhythm of action is very important; indeed, it is essential for real accuracy.

LEARNING THE OFF BREAK

This is a throw but will give the feeling of the proper wrist action for the off break when bowled

SWERVE

GRIP FOR IN-SWINGER

GRIP FOR OUT-SWINGER

Given the right conditions, i.e., a ball with some shine on it, the right wind, or a heavy atmosphere, nearly all bowlers, if their action is right, can make the ball swerve. But swerve in itself is of little value unless it is combined with control of length and direction. A young bowler must make up his mind which swerves he wants to bowl, "out" or "in", i.e., to the off or to the leg, and then set his field for it and stick to it. He should not try to bowl the other swerve, except perhaps very occasionally as a surprise ball; it is impossible to set the field for both swerves.

If the swerve is to be effective, it must be bowled to a full length and straight enough to force the batsman to play at it.

Though the bowler may find it easier to "move" the ball in than out, he may well also find that he is paying too high a price for it by the sacrifice of control in length and direction. Inaccurate in-swing is bound to be expensive; moreover, it involves an unwarrantable risk for the close-in fielders. It is also more difficult for the latter to catch the edged ball off in-swing than for slips and gully to take similar chances from out-swing.

The Out Swerve

Grip

The seam of the ball should be slightly "canted", so that at the moment of delivery it will lie in the direction of first slip. The two first fingers will be on top of the ball and on each side of the seam; the right **side** of the thumb will be on the bottom side of the seam directly beneath them.

Action

The principles of the Basic Action already described hold good, but in his wind-up the bowler should slightly exaggerate the turn of his shoulder on the batsman, and in his follow-through the right hand should swing more down and across to finish close to his left thigh. In releasing the ball he should feel the two first fingers move on behind it and the angle of the wrist kept constant for as long as possible.

The In-Swerve

Grip

The seam of the ball will be "canted" slightly towards fine leg. The second finger will lie along the inner side of the seam with the first finger more or less parallel to it; the **ball** of the thumb will be on the bottom side of the seam more or less directly beneath them.

Action

In the delivery stride the front foot will land slightly to the off side of the right foot, and the arch of the back should be slightly exaggerated.

The arm must come over as high, i.e. as close to the head, as possible, and instead of swinging across the body must come down in front of it and finish by the right thigh.

Again, the first two fingers should move on behind the ball as long as possible.

It is easier to bowl the in-swerve from wide on the crease, but the wider the point of delivery, the earlier will the ball tend to swerve and the easier will it therefore be to play.

BOWLING TACTICS

The first job of a bowler is to attack and to keep on attacking until the scoreboard, the clock or his Captain's orders force him to fall back on defence.

He must always have a clear picture of how he wants his field placed for this attack when he first goes on, but this field must be elastic and he must be prepared to adjust it according to the state of the game or the particular batsman opposed to him.

So long as he is bowling accurately enough to keep the batsmen on the defensive, close-up attacking positions such as silly mid-off and close short legs may be justified, especially if the pitch is lifting and taking spin. But unless he is accurate, those positions, especially the close legs, are not justified; for they are of no use to stop hard hits from bad balls and may well prove dangerous for the fielders who occupy them.

The general distribution of his field must always be determined by the bowler's intended normal line of attack; he must make up his mind where he wants to bowl and stick to it. Control of direction is quite as important as control of length for effective field placing. The more he is turning or swinging the ball, the more can his field be concentrated on the side to which that turn or swing is operating. He must at all costs avoid "half-way" fielders, too deep to save one, and not too deep enough to cut off four. The faster and truer the wicket, the more is the bowler justified in making some experiments in his attack on the batsman; the slower and more difficult it is, the more he must concentrate on accuracy of length and direction. In attacking every new batsman he should aim at making him play and, if possible, play forward at, every ball. This is especially true if he is entrusted with the new ball; it is criminal to "waste the shine" by allowing the batsmen to watch the ball go by or to play it comfortably off the back foot.

THE FAST BOWLER

The fast bowler has, by virtue of his pace, rather more latitude of length than the medium paced and much more than the slow bowler, but control of direction for him is essential. If he bowls to leg, he is pretty sure to be expensive in byes, whilst if he bowls too wide on the off the batsman need not play at him and he will be wearing himself out for nothing. He must bowl straight and make the batsman play.

An occasional extra fast ball short of its normal length may produce results, especially on very fast wickets or against a batsman who does not relish pace. But in general he should bowl a "full" length and remember that a yorker or even a very full half-volley is a valuable weapon, particularly against a batsman who has just come in.

He must keep his arm as high as possible; for a high arm means life off the pitch and also makes for control of direction.

He must realise that, both for sustained life and for accuracy, rhythm is the secret, and he must never strive for pace at the expense of this rhythm and control.

Most young fast bowlers take too long a run; eleven or twelve yards is quite long enough. The run must never be a rush, but a smooth and gradual acceleration; throughout it he should feel that his body is tidy and balanced.

The follow-through after delivering the ball should be full and vigorous.

He must try not to "bowl himself out" in his first spell, remembering that he may well have to come on again for a second or even a third effort, perhaps at a crucial period of the match.

He must take a pride in getting physically fit before the season starts and keeping himself fit throughout it. He must look after his feet and may be well advised to wear two pairs of socks.

Even more than other bowlers he must keep a tight grip on himself throughout the game, neither becoming excited and therefore wild, if things go right for him, nor depressed and therefore lifeless if they go wrong. Above all he must be properly shod.

THE MEDIUM PACE BOWLER

For medium pace bowlers accuracy and consistency are the first essentials. They will of course hope to reinforce this with such variety in swing, spin and change of pace as they can command, but never at the price of losing their general control. The truer the pitch, the more will the medium pace bowler have to rely on wearing the batsman down by accuracy or on luring him to make a rash or false stroke by slight changes of pace. He should make intelligent use of the width of the crease, thus altering the angle of his attack. Similarly, an occasional ball bowled from a foot or two behind the crease may bring results, provided he makes sure of giving it enough air to bring the batsman out on to his front foot.

He must always be using his brains in watching each batsman and trying to assess his strength and weakness. Some batsmen are obviously stronger on the off side than on the on, and of others the opposite is true. Some are naturally impetuous and hate being pinned down; others are essentially defensive but may be trapped by suitable temptation into attempting the attacking strokes of which they are not master.

He must be prepared to adjust his field to each batsman and indeed sometimes between two batsman in at the same time. For one he may be justified in setting a close attacking field, whilst the other may demand an inner and outer ring, the inner to save the single and the outer to stop the "four". The state of the game may at times demand that he should bowl defensively and he must then summon up all his tenacity to "shut up an end". He will be wise to concentrate his line and his field on the off side. Defensive bowling at and near the leg stump, of which he will see much in first-class cricket today, demands a high degree of accuracy and a specialized skill in the leg fielders: without these it is unlikely to be effective and may well prove highly expensive.

THE SPIN BOWLER

The Leg Spinner

The job of the leg spinner is essentially to attack, and to do so he must bowl straight, i.e. at or very close to the leg stump and he must keep the ball well up. He must expect, and indeed want, to be driven. On fast true pitches he must hope to deceive the batsman by slight changes of pace in a rather higher and slower trajectory. On dead grounds he must bowl a little faster, push the ball through, and above all never drop it short. On difficult pitches when the ball is really turning, accuracy of length is everything: his natural spin and the pitch should do the rest.

The googly, if bowled accurately, is very valuable, but it should be used sparingly and as an element of surprise. If bowled too often it loses much of its threat and may also well lead to the loss of ability to spin the ball from leg.

A stout heart and a cool head are essentials for the leg spinner; he must be prepared to be hit, and recognize that there are days when nothing will go right, but if he will stick to his craft and keep the ball up, he will often win a match for his side.

The Off Spinner

On fast true wickets the tactics of the off spinner are approximately the same as for the medium pace bowler, but his normal line of attack will be just outside the off stump, his pace will be slightly slower and his flight slightly higher than they will be on a wicket that is helping him. He should bowl over the wicket.

When the pitch really helps his spin, he will bowl round the wicket, thus greatly increasing his chance of getting l.b.w. decisions. He should still bowl at or near the off stump, but the sharp break which he should in these conditions be able to produce, will mean that his field should be largely concentrated on the on side. He will now push the ball through slightly faster but keep it well up. The worst crime for an off spinner is to drop the ball short so that the batsman can hook it without risk. Accuracy in length and direction is much more important on difficult pitches than the extra amount of spin which he may feel encouraged to attempt.

FIELDING

A boy who does not do his utmost to make himself as good as he can in the field does not really deserve the name of cricketer, and in no one branch of the game is the reward for practice and hard work more certain. Apart from regular practices run by captains and coaches, boys can do a great deal by practising in pairs to improve their ground fielding, catching and throwing. Even by himself a boy can get valuable practice by throwing a solid rubber ball at a mark on a wall and moving quickly to take it cleanly on the rebound.

Though in time he may well wish, or be required, to "specialise", every young cricketer should learn, and be prepared, to field in any position.

POSITION OF READINESS FOR CLOSE TO THE WICKET FIELDER

Head still and mind concentrated on each ball—Knees and hips well bent—Feet comfortably apart, weight evenly distributed—Hands relaxed and ready.

As in batting and bowling, so in fielding, concentration is vital. A fielder must expect—and should want—*every* ball to come to him. This concentration is hard work, but it can be built up into a habit. Once you gain some confidence and pride in your fielding, it will greatly increase your enjoyment of the game. After all, in any given match you may have little chance, or may fail, to distinguish yourself as batsman or bowler, but as long as your side is in the field, you may as a fielder at any moment influence the whole course of the game.

Really good and aggressive fielding is a tremendous support to bowlers and can cramp and unsettle the opposing batsmen.

The better you learn to field, the more sure you can be of being able to contribute to every match, and the more you will enjoy your cricket.

Defensive Fielding Positions

Heels together toes apart Fingers pointing downwards. Head down watching ball into hands.

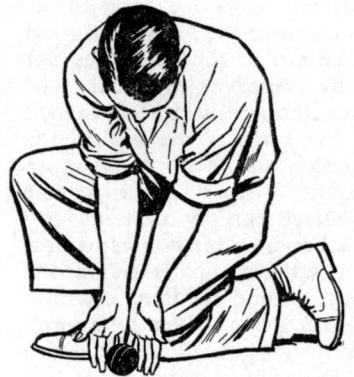

Right foot and left leg form long barrier at right angles to line of ball. Head down and on line of ball.

STOPPING THE BALL

The fielder's first job is to stop the ball, always, if possible, with his hands, but, if that fails, with some part of his body.

To make sure of doing this you must:

(1) Get on to the line of the ball as soon as possible.

(2) Get down, really down, with hands together and your whole body behind the ball and your head low and steady over your hands.

(3) Keep your fingers pointing down and not outwards towards the ball.

(4) Watch, really watch, the ball into your hands and never look up until it is securely in them.

1 Moving In

Body slightly forward and perfectly balanced ready to accelerate in any direction—

Hands "at the ready"—

"ATTACKING" FIELDING

To field well you must learn not only how to stop the ball but how to return it as quickly and accurately as possible. By so doing the fielder makes run-getting difficult and sometimes can get a wicket by a run-out.

The chief principles in this attacking technique are:

(1) Be on the move towards and watching the batsman as the ball is bowled, with your body balance slightly forward and ready to accelerate in any direction.

2 Getting Down

Right foot about to land on the line of the ball and at right angles to it—
Body turning sideways with balance over right foot—
Head well forward—

(2) Get on to the line of the ball as quickly as possible.

(3) Get down on the line of the ball with your body sideways and with hands down just in front of your right foot

3 RECOVERING THE BALL

—Hands must be right down just in front of the right foot before the ball arrives

—Knees and hips fully bent

—Head right down over right foot with eyes watching the ball

—Left foot eased

which is at right angles to that line. All the weight is on this foot and the left foot is carried away to a point of natural balance.

(4) Keep your head down and watch the ball right into your hands.

In this position the body is naturally placed for:—

4 AIMING THE THROW

Right arm with wrist cocked travelling straight back to a point behind right shoulder.
Left arm pointing at target
Head steady with eyes full on target
Body sideways with weight beginning to be transferred on to left leg

THE THROW

Good throwing is the spearhead of attack in the field. For fast and accurate throwing you should, from the attacking position:

(1) Carry your right arm, with wrist cocked, straight back until it is in line with your right shoulder, at the same time:

5 THE FOLLOW THROUGH

The head has led into the line of the throw—
Right arm and shoulder have followed through straight down the line—
Weight now fully transferred on to the left foot—

(2) Throw your left hand straight towards the wicket at which you are aiming. This acts as a rudder and is most important for control of direction.

(3) Keep your head as still as possible, with eyes fixed on the target.

(4) Aim at the wicket keeper's head, never at the stumps.

(5) Follow through with your right shoulder and arm, which at the end of the throw should be pointing straight at the target.

THE CLOSE-IN FIELDERS

All close-in fielders should watch the bat, except first slip and leg-slip who should watch the ball. For sighting the ball quickly and for quick movement in any direction their "position of readiness" should be as shown on page 73.

(1) Legs comfortably apart, with weight evenly distributed between the balls of both feet.

(2) Both knees and hips well bent; it is always easier to rise than to stoop.

(3) Hands relaxed in front of and between the knees, with fingers pointing more or less down. The forearms should be free and not resting on the thighs.

(4) Head still and mind concentrated on each ball.

To sustain this concentration throughout an innings means a constant effort of will, but remember how often it is just when this concentration has failed that the vital chance comes. A slip cradle is a valuable aid for close in fielders, but excellent practice can be obtained if two fielders will face a wall at a distance of some four or five yards and a third, standing behind them, will throw a hard rubber ball to be caught as it rebounds off the wall.

CATCHING

More catches are missed by failure to get into the proper position for catching than by failure of the hands to close on the ball. (*See facing page*).

The catcher's aim should be to:

(1) Not move till he has sighted the ball, and then to move as quickly as possible on to the line to a point where he can catch it approximately level with his face; this is specially important with high catches.

(2) Once there, keep balanced and still and really watch the ball.

(3) Spread, but never tense, the fingers and receive the ball in the "web" at the base of them. They will then automatically close.

(4) Let the hands "give" with the ball.

FIELDING

Watching the Ball

— Head still and eyes on the ball
— Body balanced
— Hands level with eyes
— Fingers slightly spread but not tensed
— Elbows well away from sides

Note: The action of making a catch starts from the time when the fieldsman first handles the ball.

The Catch Made

The head and eyes have followed the ball into the hands—

The hands "ride" with the ball which is caught and held just below the throat—

f

Here are one or two final points for all fielders.

Always watch your captain and the bowler in case either of them wants you to alter your position. They should be able to get this done without "advertising" it to the batsmen.

In order to save overthrows always "back-up", and in doing so try, if you are fielding near the wicket, to get well back from it, for unless you do, you cannot see or cover the ball if it is deflected.

Be sure you are properly shod.

PRACTISING THROWING AND FIELDING

WICKET KEEPING

The position of wicket-keeper is the most important in the field. Not only does he get more chances of dismissing the batsman than any other fielder, but he is the focus of the whole side's fielding, and on his agility and "tidiness" depends to a great extent the look of the side in the field. What is more, he can be a tremendous support to his bowlers and to his captain.

EQUIPMENT

A wicket-keeper must, of course, be properly padded, but he must realize that his legs are only his second line of defence and should never come into play unless his hands have failed him.

He should wear a pair of "inners" under his gloves and he may reinforce them with plasticine along the base of his fingers. His gloves should fit him comfortably, but not tightly, and should always be pulled right on so that his fingers are well home within the stalls. A "box" is an essential protection and a reinforcement to his confidence.

But by far the most important item in his "equipment" is an alert and determined mind, concentrated on every ball and expecting every ball to come to him, however sure the batsman seems of playing it or however certain it seems that it will hit the wicket.

POSITION

He must stand either right up or well back—never halfway. How far he stands back will depend on the pace of the bowling and of the wicket. But when standing back, his aim will be so to position himself as to take the length ball just after it begins to drop after pitching.

The Stance

Left foot behind middle stump. Right foot in line with left. Heels of both feet eased off ground. Hands pointing down with fingers nearly touching ground. Body right down, with knees and hips fully bent. Head looking straight down the wicket from just behind the stumps. Feet wide enough apart for comfort but not so wide as to restrict speed of movement.

STANCE

His weight must be equally balanced between his two feet, with body right down and eyes just higher than the stumps. His left foot should be behind the middle stump and both feet should point more or less down the wicket. His hands should be pointing down and his head must be kept as still as possible. He must get down and stay down unless and until he is certain that he must rise to take the ball.

TAKING THE BALL

His feet will move only so far as is necessary to bring his head and body across behind the line of the ball. His line of balance should always be forward and, when taking balls on the off and leg side, slightly inwards towards the wicket: a slight pointing inwards of his outside foot will help him to achieve this. He must never move *back* from the wicket. He should always try to take the ball in his gloves, forming a relaxed cup with the fingers pointing down. His hands should "ride" with the ball as they take it but, once securely taken, he should bring it back to the wicket ready for the opportunity of a stump.

TAKING A RISING BALL JUST OUTSIDE THE OFF STUMP

Head and body full behind the line of the ball.

The hands, with fingers pointing down, take the ball close to the wicket and right below the eyes.

Taking a Leg Ball

The left foot has moved over but not back, and the right has followed it. Body balance forward right behind line of the ball. Fingers pointing down.

Keeping Down

The batsman has driven the ball on the half volley but the wicket-keeper is still right down and would only have risen if he had seen it rise off the pitch.

STUMPING

Most stumpings are missed because the wicket-keeper looks at the bat instead of the ball or looks up before he has taken it or snatches at it through over-eagerness. He must at all cost resist these temptations and concentrate on taking the ball securely.

TAKING RETURNS FROM THE FIELD

He must move as fast as he can to get directly behind and close up to the stumps, facing straight down the line of the return. If the return is wide, he must get on to the line as quickly as possible. He must keep down and watch the ball right into his hands. He must never look up at the running batsman. However wild the return he must try to take it tidily and never be content just to stop it with his pads.

He must take trouble to return the ball, either an easy lobbed catch direct to the bowler, or on the relay system, to a nearby fielder. It is a crime to make the bowler stoop to receive the ball.

PRACTICE

It is excellent practice to get a friend to bowl or throw the ball at you, varying its length and direction at a range of 10 to 15 yards; better still, if you can get another friend to stand in front with a bat and play at and miss (and occasionally hit) the ball. Always have a wicket for this practice and concentrate on positioning yourself quickly, taking the ball correctly as already described and bringing the ball back quickly to the stumps.

Even by yourself you can practise by throwing a rubber ball at short range against a wall and taking the rebound behind the stumps.

To concentrate on every ball throughout a long innings means very hard work and to be able to do so a wicket-keeper must be fit and really determined. But it is a grand challenge, and if he can meet it, he will be of incalculable value to his side.

CAPTAINCY

A captain's first duty is to lead. Through his study and understanding of the game he should know what he wants to do and how to get it done. He must understand his team, both as cricketers and as individuals; to get the best out of them they must trust him and know that he will always put them first and himself last. He must, by his keenness and determination, set an example to the others. If he is to inspire confidence in them, he must make them feel that he believes in them and relies on their giving of their best. He must keep cheerful, however badly things are going, and above all he must encourage, especially those who are out of form or out of luck. Discipline is, of course, essential, but the best discipline comes from a feeling of loyalty to, and confidence in the captain. There may be times when he feels that one of his players is not giving of his best, but it is much better to tackle him in a quiet talk before or after the match than during play: on the field only idleness, casualness or bad cricket manners should get the rough side of his tongue.

A captain should be continually thinking about cricket and trying to learn from his experience. Though on the field he should always be in sole command, he should at all times be ready and anxious to discuss his problems with older and more experienced cricketers and to learn from them. There is never any end to what a captain can learn.

OFF THE FIELD

The duties and responsibilities of a school captain will naturally vary in different types and sizes of school, but there are some that must be common to all. He must see that the best possible use is made of such practice facilities as are available. He must be prepared, if necessary, to get his men to roll the match and net wickets, especially the latter. He must be sure that they all take their net practice really keenly and seriously and this applies to the bowlers just as much as to batsmen.

Nothing reflects a captain's keenness and example more

surely than the fielding of his side. If they really mean business and if regular and well-organised practices are the rule, any school side can learn to field well and this makes a tremendous difference, not only to the bowlers, but to the general confidence and morale of the whole team.

A captain should see that his XI turns out as smartly as possible and in this should set an example himself. He must see, too, that they look after their equipment properly; this applies especially to bowlers keeping their boot-nails clear of mud.

He should insist on their turning up in good time for any engagement, whether a match or practice, and remind them that in home matches it is their duty to look after the visiting side, especially at meals! He must, of course, himself be on the ground in time to welcome them on arrival and he should stay on it to see them off.

He should know the Laws of Cricket and the notes which accompany them, and before a match starts he should be sure that he and his opposing captain are clear about the hours of play, the times of intervals, and the custom of the ground as to boundaries. At the end of play a word of thanks to the umpires, the scorers and the groundsman is never out of place.

OUT IN THE FIELD

Before he takes the field, a captain should have thought out his general plan of campaign and should have his field placing for each bowler clear in his head, with a thought for any adjustments which may be necessary for a left-handed batsman. He will, if he is wise, have "rehearsed" these in "match fielding practices", and a well-trained side should fall into place in the field with very little direction from their captain. He should also have trained them to keep their eyes on him in the field so that he can make slight alterations in their positions without "advertising" it to the batsmen.

It is, of course, essential that his general plan of campaign and the field placing that goes with it should be "elastic". He must be prepared to adjust it as the game develops, and this ability to keep his mind alert all the time and to meet, and even to anticipate, the changes in the game's balance is one of the most important qualities in good captaincy.

His first aim will be to attack and to keep on attacking until he is forced to defend. He will presumably start with the two bowlers who can make best use of the new ball, and if one or both of them is fast, so much the better. But he must be careful not to "bowl them into the ground" in their first spell. They must be able to come back. If he has a good spin bowler, he should bring him on pretty soon, for most school batsmen are troubled by spin, especially if it is from the leg. Moreover, variety of attack between the two ends is of itself valuable. He must beware of running through all his possible bowlers before bringing on again the more dangerous of them.

The better the wicket and the more easily runs seem to be coming, the more will he be justified in experimenting with his bowling in order to get a wicket. Under these conditions it is probably true that any change is better than no change. The more difficult the wicket, the more he should rely on his most accurate bowlers, adjuring them to bowl straight and to keep the ball well up.

He must be alert to alter his field placing according to the state of the game, or even between two batsmen who are together at the wicket. For one, a wholly attacking field may be justified, whilst for his partner he may have to set his field defensively. An attacking field should always be set for each new batsman. Half-way places very seldom make sense. He should remember that, when placing his field on the leg side, not more than two fielders are allowed behind the popping crease. He should always be ready to listen to a bowler's views about the disposition of his field, but the final decision must be his. He should always be trying to gauge a batsman's weakness and suggest it to his bowlers.

He must always be encouraging his bowlers and fielders, especially when things are going wrong, and must never allow them to think that he himself is rattled or has lost heart. Optimism and courage are great qualities for all cricketers, and above all for captains.

FROM THE PAVILION

A captain is lucky if he can settle his side, or most of it, early in the season, for this should mean a regular batting order and the sooner he can determine it and the more he can stick to it the better. There may be times when it is advisable to alter the normal order, as when runs have to be made against time, but he should remember that nothing puts a side behind the clock so surely as losing wickets, while as long as wickets are in hand, it is possible at any time to order a quickening of the batting attack.

To bat or not to bat? There may be circumstances under which a captain must consider putting the other side in: he may feel that his team have been unsettled by their journey and need time to get adjusted: he may believe that his bowlers can take decisive advantage of a hot sun on a wet wicket: (but the mere fact that it has rained is no reason for thinking that the wicket will be difficult: indeed, the wetter the wicket and the more likely therefore it is to cut up, the less should he hesitate about batting first). Or again where the time limit for the match is comparatively short and he believes in his team's superiority, he may well feel that to field first will give him the best chance of forcing a win. It will certainly save him the difficult decision of timing his declaration. But in general it is true that it is easier to save runs in the last innings than to make them, and the younger and the more inexperienced the cricketers, the more this is the case. In deciding to bat first he is far more likely to be right than wrong.

A captain should insist on his batsmen being padded-up and ready to go in with plenty of time to spare. If they can have a few minutes' practice at a net, so much the better.

If he sits with his team and watches the play closely, he may often be able to say a valuable word to those about to bat, even if it is only "I shouldn't try to hit that leg spinner against the break," or "that third man is fat and can't throw; there's a run to him, if he stays as deep as he is." But he should beware of fussing his batsmen and of trying to tell them how to play. A cheery "good luck: watch the ball" is as good a last word as any.

UMPIRING

Good umpiring is of the first importance in cricket. Bad umpiring can ruin a match. Boys may often have to umpire and they should regard it not as something to be avoided if possible or at best as a rather boring necessity, but as part of their service to the game and, incidentally, it can be very enjoyable. Umpiring is not only a job to be done, but an opportunity for learning all the time. The umpire must be prepared to think hard about what he sees at such close quarters and so add to his personal experience, lessons not only of technique but of tactics and character.

The first requirement in an umpire is obviously that he should know the Laws of Cricket and the Notes which accompany them. To do this he cannot do better than study the handbook *Know the Game Cricket!* Price 25p, published for the M.C.C. by E.P. Publishing Ltd., in which the official code is supplemented by a number of explanatory drawings and comments, covering not only the Laws themselves but the various signals which an umpire should use. It is essential that he should know these signals and make them properly, and he should make sure that the scorer acknowledges them.

In this short chapter no attempt will be made to cover the Laws individually, with one exception: The L.B.W. Law is undoubtedly the most difficult and important which an umpire has to interpret, and this will be dealt with at the end. But here are some general principles which all umpires should keep in mind.

Before the match starts, they should agree on the boundaries and should know the hours fixed for play and for the intervals. This will of course equally apply to any who may relieve the first umpires during the game. There should also be agreement as to the clock or watch registering the official time. It is the business of the umpires to be out in the field two or three minutes before play is actually due to begin, whether it is at the start of an innings or after an interval, even if it means cutting short their own tea!

Each umpire should take with him some means of registering the number of balls bowled in an over. Much the simplest is a set of six pebbles which he transfers one at a time from one hand or one pocket to another as each ball is bowled.

The umpire at the bowler's end must stand directly behind the wicket so that he is looking straight down the pitch. He may sometimes be asked by a bowler to stand a little way back from the wicket but should only do so if he is satisfied that his view is completely unaffected. He should always give the batsman guard from directly over the wicket. That is the place from which he will give his L.B.W. decisions and a batsman who asks for guard "from where the bowler bowls" is only exposing his ignorance.

The Square-leg umpire should stand directly in line with the popping crease. If, as the match progresses, he finds that a low sun is in his eyes, he may ask the fielding captain's agreement to his crossing over to the off-side.

When the ball is being returned to the bowler's wicket, the umpire there must get out of the way and, especially if there seems a chance of a run-out, must move quickly to one side or other of the wicket, a little way back from it and parallel with the popping crease.

In deciding on an appeal for a catch at the wicket, he must use his eyes as well as his ears: a click may be caused by the ball flicking a pad or a pad-strap, even by a sprung bat-handle. A batsman can be caught off his hand when holding the bat but not off his wrist.

THE L.B.W. LAW

For a batsman to be out under this Law the following conditions must be fulfilled.

(1) The ball must have pitched on a line between wicket and wicket or on the off-side of it. A batsman cannot be L.B.W. to any ball that has pitched outside the leg stump.

(2) The ball must, but for the intervention of the batsman's person, have been going to hit the wicket.

(3) The part of the batman's person which it hits must be, when it is hit, between wicket and wicket.

In applying these tests the umpire must take into account the angle of the ball after it pitches, i.e., whether it is breaking enough to miss the wicket or rising sharply enough to go over it. A ball may hit the batsman at a level well above the stumps but be dropping so sharply that it would hit the wicket. In that case it is out.

The further the batsman's front leg is down the pitch when the ball hits it, the more likely is the ball to miss the wicket if it has begun to break after pitching or to swing before pitching.

In giving an L.B.W. decision an umpire has to weigh up all these factors and many of the best umpires take an appreciable time before they give it. Unless he is quite clear that all these conditions have, in fact, been fulfilled, he must give the batsman "the benefit of the doubt."

To umpire conscientiously and well means ceaseless concentration and that is very hard work. But both sides will have cause to be grateful to you, if you face up to it.

MORE ADVANCED CRICKET

For more detailed and advanced study of all departments of the game the reader is recommended to study the *M.C.C. Cricket Coaching Book*. This has been written for and issued with the official backing of the M.C.C. It is illustrated with a large number of very carefully selected action photographs of great players and many specially drawn action sketches. *William Heinemann Ltd.*

CRICKET COACHING CHARTS

A series of six colourful charts designed so that each covers a particular skill in the game.

1. BATTING: showing the grip, stance, forward and backward defence.
2. BATTING: off driving, on driving, and moving out.
3. BATTING: cuts off the back foot, hits to the leg.
4. BOWLING: the sequence action and grips for different breaks.
5. WICKET KEEPING: stance and taking a leg ball.
6. FIELDING: position of readiness, throw in and catching.

Six charts, size 20 in. by 30 in., price 90p.